She Lives in Music

Andrea "Vocab" Sanderson

FlowerSong BOOKS

FlowerSong Books
McAllen, Texas 78501

Copyright © 2020 by Andrea Sanderson

ISBN: 978-1-7345617-1-5

Published by FlowerSong Books
in the United States of America.
www.flowersongbooks.com

Set in Arial

Cover art by Mac Shelton
Typeset by Matthew Revert

She Lives in Music

Andrea "Vocab"
Sanderson

Table of Contents

Author's Prelude

For my 37th year of life, I choose to celebrate with poem and song lyrics related to music genres and the way the music influenced my life over the years. From hope to heartbreak, I traverse this emotional terrain with wobbly legs and heavy footsteps. No journey is easy, but I am leaving space for the music to speak through my pen at every corner. I couldn't possibly cover it all. Sometimes it is very literal; I explore musicians and their influences on my music. Other times, I use language itself to create a melodic landscape for my heart to tell my story.

There are Endnotes if you flip to the end to give some context for my dramatic musings. Overall, I hope the sights and sounds resonate with your personal passion for music and it bears witness to the flavor and music that lives inside of you as well.

Press

play.

Electric Reign

Electric heat poured out on pandemonium at full capacity. A high octave trill tolls over a standing stadium of adoration. The Artist salaciously licks his guitar strings, with tantric fingers and tongue teasing the room till hypnosis occurs. A low feline purr follows, as slender hips swivel with the magnetic pulse of the band. His petite body becomes a paintbrush. He thrusts wet bristles onto the canvas. A feverish stroke that slathers the soul in tertiary color. We all become a part of the masterpiece he is creating. Nothing escapes his touch. Nothing escapes his gaze. His voice navigates the air like a ship in calm waters. We are drowning in the leagues of his deep, immersed into a satisfaction so sensual. We are billowing timeless lyrics that transport us out of body intergalactic. Each note, a dove released into a chorus that surrounds us. The energy of connection penetrates the atmosphere; and we are tuned just like his guitar. We hum with this lavish vibration being swept away into a surreal feeling. Living in the moment, because we've been seduced into surrender. We want the seduction of this symphonic rapture. We climb the walls for you. You give us every genre. You quench our thirst with a crush velvet mysterious caress. You tuck passion underneath our skin and we perspire it. We let go with you, because you've channeled freedom into the chords of your music. We are your *Beautiful Ones*, adorned with your *Purple Rain* royalty, sweet Prince.

Origins of an Arkestra Leader

Birmingham bebop baby, you were born unfettered and future minded.

You were born with the fine-grained soot of pyramids swirling in the cosmic dust of your brown, brown skin.

Sun baked and blazing you were birthed in free form with fingers like an acrobat, with fingers like the paws of a wild cat. With the impulse and reflexes of a glittering obsidian panther, or a jaguar, imprinted in your DNA. You had sitar strings wrapped around your spinal column. You were delivered to this earth with ivory keys etched into your irises and the blueprint for a bounty of music to be unleashed from your architect hands.

You were awaiting the ancient to speak through you, a conduit for melodious chaos. Apophis was your muse and your nemesis too. His snakeskin the rhythm and blues that rattles like a tail in your troubadour heart space.
We all marvel at how you were able to painstakingly create. All along you were sealing the fate of silence in your organized noize, swallowing the void. A jazz ravishing, foretelling a future yet unseen.

You were tabulating and formulating the immeasurable equation up and down the scale, traversing interstellar, if we could accelerate to your dimension we would inquire:

If you're not a myth, whose reality are you? If you're not a myth, whose reality are you?

You put the virtue in virtuoso, and the soul power in

Afrofuturism.

You were piloting spaceships with George Clinton, telling us all to vibrate

higher. You wore celestial attire before Andre 3000.

Indeed you are the prototype, the protégé, the

prodigy, the protagonist of pro-blackness that we

witness on display. I will raise a black fist as we put your

art on replay, replay, replay.

Invocation to Sun Ra

My words are merely a *Prelude for Stargazers.*

A lullaby intended for you who let leaflets of sound drop a reservoir of melisma from your honeyed lips. The melody is intended as an *Opus In Springtime.* A clarion whisper from the Mayan Temples intended to summon your saturated soulfulness.

May a path be clear from the Duat tonight. Bring us your *Enlightenment Hours After.*

You show me *Images In a Mirror* reflective of the time. Accomplished pianist brings us a *Jazz in Silhouette*; your euphony orbits us like *Saturn's* rings.

Your music coerces us with Velvet textures. Your mood foretelling like a *Horoscope.*

Your song a zodiac elixir. Your psalms a poetic mixture.

A chromatic chameleon, a cerulean soundscape leading to a dusky violet *Blues at Midnight.*

Come to us brilliant, come to us orchestral, come to us an Ankh, symbolic of life, even after yours has ended we are still bemused by you.

Fire
Fruit

Give me an artist whose life hasn't been spoon fed, who had to scrap for bread, dang near fought from the dead. It's been said that, we write our best when we've emotionally bled. So, we have been led down a path of pain to spread our hearts out on a canvas of life. Gobble up all the turmoil and strife. My sorrow is ripe for the picking. Now that's a new type of *Strange Fruit,* plump with nectar-bittersweet juice.

Who made you feel it deep within? Who brought the connection that lured you in? Whose web spins and when you are in, you don't struggle to be free? Who is it baby, who is it baby? Was it Sarah Vaughn or Ella Fitz? Was it Nina Simone, with her pouty lips? Or Chaka Khan? Patti Patti, Miss Mahalia, or Janis? Sade, with her hypnotic hips?

> Tell me: whose fruit have you
> bitten?

All these ladies got my kryptonite, every time they step to a mic! And at night when I can't clear my head, can't calm my heart, their voice is a torch from a subtle spark. My dark can't hold them, but my belly can. I eats their fire fruit and understands. I swallow the pyre and my tongue is ignited with their tune. I eat their fire fruit, until I am consumed.

Half to
Hathaway

I was giving half of my soul away to the sound of Donny
Hathaway.

He put lavender creases in my pillow and a fantasia of burgundy blues wilted my
roses on Valentine's Day this year. It was about two in the afternoon. I spilled my
cup of tears for the fears of lonelys. Only eyes could drink this liquor so drunk am I
with pain. Only agony could do me quicker. Take me from this mind frame - was my
meditation and prayer.

> Lord, please pay my toll and fare so I can take a trip from my burden
> and care.

I am so tired of pleading for romantic justice for just this occasion. I stare off the mantel
out the glass to the past from the picture of myself and someone else whose eyes knew
the meaning of abandon. I became random to his embrace and my face featureless like
other strangers he didn't know.

So, he began to show me no attention. Failed to mention words or talk with touching.
Never even bothered brushing me off. His dismissal was a missile that hit me soft. His
dismissal was a missile that hit me soft. Caught me right in the chamber with no warning
of danger. There was no remainder of me, or any casualty victim to retrieve.

I stood defenseless and now only my spirit grieves in remembrance of me. Only the
picture believes that we were ever side by side. Donny now allies with my aching voice
for making the choice to be *giving up*... His voice dug into me like a shovel, coupled with
the thought of that man, and I began to understand the meaning of soul. From present

to old, the truth of joy and pain, the definition of surrender to the song as it reclaims our emotion explains our being. I was sound seeing the victory of a battle fought to preserve, the intensity of every thought heard.

Donny, you gave my soul back through your
words.

You whispered the duplication of my heart. What you sang was a statue. You modeled the attributes somehow chiseled the parts. Died before your time, music topping the charts. I could cart around vintage vinyl in denial that you are gone, because your presence in the music is so strong. Your presence in the music still carries on. Your voice is a shovel and you are buried so deep within me. We are both gone to that place in space where music lives long after the song ends.

I was giving half of my soul away to the sound of Donny
Hathaway.

The Wandering Phantom

In dreams he came to
me
        face half masked, concealing some of his
        intentions.

The beams in his retinas
alluring,
        traces of his past now hidden, unrevealing his darkest
        dimension.

My dreams welcomed the
haunting.

        Spaces of a path to my heart unveiling my deepest
        decision.

It seems the phantom is
lingering

        Yet I wake and bask in the memory, reveling in the remnants of inner
        visions.

The Sunny Sound of Music

Ray (Re), A drop of golden sun
sung out

Marigold melody of light Vibrating intonation
throughout the body and atmosphere.

You spun out of my heart a tune. You became a
magnet of attraction for joy from my lungs.

There is no longer a place for darkness
within. My abode is one of resonating
radiance, From the branches of my arms
To the root position of my tonic chord.

You soar out of me, sunshine. Blind my lips from
negative tones I cannot speak
of bleakness again.

I cannot hum any other hue than
you, My magical pitch of
platinum.

A
Duet

Part 1: Kind of Blue

I will not change my color, for I have found the hue that suits me
deeply. *So What*, if you cannot understand. I have wet my reed
and let the emotion bleed deep into my horn.

I have found the frequency of forlorn, sitting
juxtapose to quarter note, tapping its toes.

It is here where I will place my prose like a single white rose on a casket
carved of the richest mahogany. I will place my prose here below a lazy
Freddie Freeloader, willfully slouching on the shoulder of melancholy. Those
ivory keys cannot tickle me with folly. I will let me lips wilt down into a frown
rubbing *Blue in Green*... Careening in a conversation only muted by
trumpeting devastation. I will let the blast blanket me - softened bebop free –
complexity-stricken chords gone crazy, over the top.

I cannot afford such a frenetic exertion of
sound.

My tongue is tightly wound against my wounded pallet, pushing
air into this instrument finding polyphony blended beautifully, to
compliment my fellow players.

We are the purveyors of melodious whispers, unrestricted by

measure. Using the mode as our muse, we captivate the frame
of meter and time, verse and rhyme. Pacing through legato we
meld with the climb.

Wide eyed, seeking the place where structure and improv align, strike
a balance supine, and *All Blues* bursts from the seams of bow and
bell. Yes, I have placed my prose here. I will eternally dwell, tipping my
hat brim to the mellow scale of composition as I proposition, Orpheus
and Apollo alike to come and sit-in with the band tonight.

Let us plot our flight into a legendary realm that exceeds comprehension and
compare. Sharp lead rippling out, *Flamenco Sketches* out like binary code, so
a spectrum of once subdued blues, folds.

Part 2: All Blues

Can we take this brass, paint it
serene? Baby, let me fade your love
Blue in Green. I used to taste your jazz.
It was so supreme. Tertiary colors
gradating the scene.

Enviously I watch. Jealousy embedded within; I listen. The way you caress
her bronze curvaceous form like passion gave you permission. You hold
her neck in submission. Whisper sweet nothings into a delicate pouty
mouthpiece. Tornadic winds begin blowing in my mind. You've creased the
corners of my heart bent. Virtually all your time is spent pressing her
buttons.

I want all or nothing. I am passionately possessive. My
gaze arrests you like the police. As I call for a cease and
desist. But you can't resist, the temptation to play with her.

I beckon for your love, but you stay Miles away. I summon
you, but you are afloat toward jagged rocks, siren swayed. I
beckon for you my love, but you stay miles away.

You foolish minstrel! Can't you see?
You blow your cool and she sets you
free.

I'm here when she goes silent. When twilight fades
into the wee hours. This art has got you captive,
under lock and key. You cower to the calling, Falling
beneath the brew and spell.

I watch envy scaling my skin like a crocodile's'
tail. You wail one last note and cloak my heart in
the dark. A riff that tears my pulp apart.

I Am the
Remix

I am the version that my ancestors alluded to in the
original.

Soul stirring vocal tracks stemming into my DNA. My
bloodline was mixed and mastered this way. The
echoes of my parents panning left to right,
transplanting from mono to stereo sounds put
together.
        I am vinyl gripped from the catalog before being laid
down, then flipped on its side to begin the instant replay.
Cause it sounded so good you had to run it back.

Mama, I carry the reverb of every word you'd pray in my southern tone,
like a Mahalia Jackson solo. I hijacked your smile hid it underneath my
cheeks. But I am big boned as Grandma Jewel, on my daddy's side.

Her pigment and posture poised over me and I wear it like an album sleeve
of pride. This artwork cover is glossy and fly. I've enclosed a bonafide
discography. I hold my father's passion for music and it's swirling in my
ebony calligraphy. He went crate digging with Ms. Elizabeth LaVern back in
1981. Love was so cool back then that it, Sly and the Family Stone, slid into
their soundtrack to produce me at the dawn of the millennium. So I flow
alternating hits from analog to digital drop. I am a sample ripped from my
parents' masterpiece, chopped into audio clips from Roberta Flack to The
Last Poets, spoken in native tongues.

Can you hear the hand stroke on the drum? I am so
Afro Blue. I am the remix. I am the remix. I am the
remix.

I have become an anthem, a downloadable edible melody.
I am whirlwind of womanhood concealing a clandestine
mystery. The matriarchs tasted a sampler of sound bites to
create me, heavenly as manna in their mouth.

But foreign tongue trips over the hip-hop tempo they are lost in the loop
of an 8-track and down beat rhythm, stumbling over the syncopation of
my flow. I've been flipped over like a cassette. My hidden gems have yet
to be discovered. Speed it up a hair, crossfade, then find a new
instrumental. Mix me with it, like a dope dance track being born on the
turntables.

My meter is smothered in soul. The Bantu and Shango know:
So I was elevated through the ancestry. Laced with the beat of
the bongos. I am the fables the ancient orators spoke of
centuries ago. Timeless as golden oldies and Negro spirituals.
My genes swing and lindy hop. Phonograph the ragtime in my spine,
crank up the bebop in my hips a notch. I am a jazzy lass with a
splash of uncensored lyrics leaking out my lips. Every part of my
anatomy is stamped explicit.
I am the remix, can you hear it? Hear me roar. From the ceiling to the floor let my
version pour out the speakers. Thumping and giving you something so fresh, so real. I
am the version of the original with mass appeal.

I am the remix. I am the remix. I am the
remix.

Jazzy
Jeff

for Charles "Easy Lee"
Peters

I'm so sentimental in my mood. A touch of
lady sings the blues: Lauryn Hill meets
Langston Hughes. Light to sparks - instant
fuse *Classic Ghetto Soul* harmonies infused -
Take great escapes to Hidden Beach for my
refuge therein lies the muse. See this dude is
Easy, laid back breezy, debonair like
Ellington and Astaire. He like my stairway to
heaven, conscience cultured brethren. I'm so
sultry siren, vibe'n with the ebb and flow. We
converse over *Free Verse* and let the *Love*
Rain Slowly, Surely. Living life *Golden*, Soul
is purely rooted in the elements of hip hop.
We spin it like a disc jockey, Jazzy Jeffrey.
Peep the story, dawn like morning glory. Jeff
meets Jilly one day in Philly, gets the feelin'.
This is the beginning of magic in the making
start recording: *Who Is Jill Scott?* They,
creating poetic and kinetic energy. Inflating
set this hope afloat, the Mojoe they invoke
Bogarts the industry. Tada! The rest is history
- so similar to you and me, such a beautiful
discovery hovering on the edge of a tipping

music scale. The artistry, it suits us well. You so Nas, *It Ain't Hard to Tell*. Force that cracks the shell, we gonna rock da bells! Magnolia bloom and yellow rose, spitting raps and penning prose, raising toasts after shows - You Noir, me Grigio. You so, I'm so.... he so, she so jazzy, yo!

Set
Adrift

It's P.M. Dawn and I am *set adrift on memory bliss of
you.*

My midnight radio dial is
staying tuned and locked into the crooning precipitation that blinks from the eye of a
quiet storm mix. There is no static, just a matrix of melodies taking effect on my mind in
waves of ambient colors and abstract patterns. Instrumentation carrousels into a sweet
swirling composition, but it's the lull of the strings that turns down my comforter tonight.
You've become the mint on my pillow top. I just can't stop taking in the sight set before
my slumbering eyes.

But If I blink you may disappear from my memory. Like ripples set forth in a pond by
skipping rocks you redirect the ebb of my waters. Falter the movement of clocks in
an animated reframe. Change the tempo of sand trickle in hourglass formation. The
metronome clicks with the drip of each grain.

You are the tribulation in my temple
tonight. You've become a requiem of light in the darkest of chambers. The alcove in my
breastbone lifts unsteadily from erratic inhalations.

But you could set my breath right with just one
beat of your heart pounding beneath the very rib cage that God abstracted my
substance from.

Now, I suppose there is a sequence to this slow dance from visual contact to
fingertip caressing, but tonight we will meld beneath the music. I will become a mario-
nette doll hanging on strings for you to tug ever so slightly. I will bow with the grace of
a ballet dancer at curtain call dangling beneath transparent chords. At the stroke of the
hour I will personify your inherent desire. Satiate you infinitely. Sway there for what is
seemingly an eternity.

Me, needing to respond to the rise and ridge in your

movements. You, propelling each swing with the ease of a

conductor.

The music peaks and sound
resonates. It is a.m. now and I am prowling the perimeters of my discovery. Wiping the
afterglow from your twilight skin with palms placed gently to your flesh and dressed in
the blanket of light spilling in from the skyline. I lean hazily on the incline of dream state.
Wishing only to slink back into the covers and recount us again. I conjure you back to
the soundtrack replaying in my mind as I float *Adrift on Memory Bliss of You.*

The
Opiate

She sips lonely like it's freshly brewed, Never stirs in sugar

cubes. Vapors rising from percolating emotions and

steeping memories, she drinks this cup empty. Friendliness

seeping from her laugh lines, smile sinking into a steaming

hot liquid of bitterness and wrinkles. Her nose crinkles like

soggy tea bags from the toil of trying... trying to be kind,

trying to unwind, trying to find segues for small talk; she just

stalks around strained like sap.

She wants to relax, but she spews words

haphazardly. Her personality doesn't shine like it used

to. Thirstily she keeps sipping cup after cup of this

bland brew. waiting for a robust flavor to bust through,

with a desire to pour out, like the spout of a boiling

kettle, but simply not remembering how to...

Verse

2

He breathes despair like filtered shorts, chokes on carcinogens at the

thought of divorce. Dispersing ringlets of sorrow from puckered lips,

clouding the air with remorse. He wants to kiss the budded lips of his

wife. He wishes she would interrupt with each puff, but strife has built

into the silence. Life has knelt into the silence...

Nowadays, that's the only thing that escapes her eyelids. No sparks strike with the matches that gather in the ashtray. He is running out of words to say, running out to buy yet another pack to smoke away his breath. He fears and inhales nothing is left. With the last drag exhaled and the cigarette laid to rest, cancerous path to his grave is paved in cherry embers and gray ashes.

Verse

3

She bleeds love like it's fiercely cut. Razor to the fragile flesh, wrist dangling up. Her arms drip out the bloodied sound her words would never speak. She slashes to get in touch with reality, but only feels the fluid from her body leak. Self-loathing crashes into her memories. She weeps suicide like an idle prayer from her sacred eyes. Hallelujahs dripping scarlet onto her naked thighs. Limbs juxtaposed like a marionette doll waving goodbye.
Sirens will wail in the
distance, But she will never
cry.

Verse

4

He laughs lonely... jokes freely
cracked, scrambled and fried. His
feathers are puffed with pride. He

clucks, mouth agape, head tilted back.

Like a hen hatching heavy chuckles

from an even heavier heart. Finishes

first impressions with a false start.

He's a rooster crowing irony and puns in every one of his

punch lines. He pecks away at people with cynicism and insults

that leave his truths undefined. Cold shoulders and snap

judgments polishes, his humor refined. Smearing yellow yokes

he plays the dirty dozens to pass the time. You will always find

him stepping on those same eggshells that blow up like land

mines.

Bass In
Between

Slick sleek as a cylinder glass polished by moonlight it stood upright beside him. Thump of jazz pumped into crescendo. He strummed satisfaction with thoughtful notes of genius. The only thing between us was the instrument of Charlie Mingus.

Tip, tap, finger snap, rift in the gift of line. Strings resonate in the vibration of holy headquarters. He was our transporter, the music supporter to our lives. He just kept finger filing, opposable thumbing, and bravado just kept humming and humming. I loved every minute of his voyage around the sun spinning us further toward Venus.

The only thing between us was the instrument
of ...

Gave the souvenir of sight on silent nights in dim lit speakeasies. Oh, how he could please the brown women rubbing elbows and patting polished toes in syncopation. The elation bringing inhibitions to half-mast as the spirits splashed down the corridors of throats. He cross-stitched complex classical and gospel below the ceilings of Café Bohemia making music float from *Fables of Faubus* such an instrumental linguist.

The only thing between us was the instrument
of...

Wave your conductor wand. Weave your fingertips to clip *Ecclesiastics*, or *Cumbia and Jazz Fusion*. Fingers move so fast it looks like optical illusions. *Pithecanthropus Erectus* gone resurrect us like Nicodemus speaking to Jesus!

The only thing between us was the instrument

of ...

I want to go down to India, swim in the Ganges River find where they sprinkled
your sacred ashes. Reconnect the splashes of avant-garde find the depth of your
melody. Hidden in the belly of your bass lines which echo through every venue
passing the signatures of time. Ironic, how they didn't even play your *Epitaph* until
10 years after you had passed. But the beloved bass will be the last to cry. I wish
you were here so you can strum the tears from the strings, cause the Children
need the music that you bring. The orchestra could clothe us as we reach a rhyth-
mic stream at its zenith. The only thing that will be between us is your instrument.

Like a gust of air encircling, like a miracle working its way to provide for us. It is
a blessed bass player, virtuoso, composer feeling his chorus. Like a dust bowl
swarming before us, until it settles in the hush of a crowded room, being consumed
by the thump of jazz being pumped in a sweet gush of crescendo play. We are
developing in the womb of music...your bass strings the umbilical cord to us the
maturing fetus. And the only thing, I mean the only thing between is your instru-
ment Charlie Mingus.

String Me
Along

Chorus

I feel the sting: Pop, break, vibrate as

you string me along

Verse

1

I wanted a duet, you weren't

ready yet. You took a solo and

walked away. You've rattled my

cage without asking.

Plucking away the life out of me one phrase at a

time. Then lay me on my belly, real still and

paralyzed. I let the song cry for you like, Jay-Z

Jaguar Wright. You keep on picking strings,

doing selfish little things offering chords

dissonant and clashing. Strings bent, the sting

won't relent. Caught in this predicament. My

heart regrets the day. You picked me up to play.

Pre
chorus

I can't counter your erratic rhythms. I stay
here... against my better judgement and
wisdom. We're out of tune, but you won't
listen.

Wish I could pitch correct this root position. Wish
you could supply what I've been missing. But aahhh

Verse
2

I don't know how much pressure
I can take.

You need to loosen me. I feel the
ache. You strike a chord. I pulsate.

In a forced frenzy against the frets. You are shredding & letting go
of the melody you once made with me. The frequency is irrational
to me. No theory can summarize. Nor surmise the key. Sometimes
it's too tight, it ain't right. Slight miscalculation causing so much
tension in our situation. So many wasted opportunities to clear up
misconceptions, misconceptions.

Pre

chorus

I can't counter your erratic rhythms. I stay

here... against my better judgement and

wisdom. We're out of tune, but you won't

listen.

Wish I could pitch correct this root position. Wish

you could supply what I've been missing. But aahhh

Bridge

You plucking on me. You

keeping strumming on me.

You just playing with me.

You keep strumming on me.

You just plucking with me.

You keep playing with me.

Awww yeah.

Queen of Swing

She's got reptilian hip rhythm and songs slither from underneath her hissing skin. She is a brown and dewy body, bathed in a *balayage* of stage lighting. She is pyre igniting by hitting the rafters with the purest beauty she can possibly muster from her inflated lungs. We will all succumb to her snake charms. Arms extended, she is hugging the reverie of the horn section. Her form physically conducting a scatting soul session. She is such a sweet little dancer. *A tisket-a-tasket, an old yellow basket,* burrows its way into the silver realistic microphone. Her tone breaking free from expectations, her tone breaking the color barriers of Jim Crow, her voice colliding with stereotypes and changing perceptions, all in one night. All in one nightclub, *Stompin' at the Savoy.* Her crown, in its' place, the Queen of Swing, graces us all. Belle of the ballroom, a blooming foliage of feathers adorning her tightly curled follicles. The molecules of her radiance showering the Philharmonic, as jazz chords trumpet-up-the balcony. No one is seated. No one is standing, everyone levitating. She is elevating the artform. Get it? Ella-vating. Nonconformist mystic, that she is. Hypnotist, is what she is, whether it's elegant Ella meets Ellington, to the duets with the dizziness of Gillespie, she is so impressive, because of the prowess of pleasure filled chords making their exodus from her parted Red Sea lips. But she be the female pharaoh, tightening her grip, enslaving us all with her music. We are whipped, stunned into silence. And whether she is descending a strand of Chick's percussionist Webb, or ascending a riff with Calloway's big band; she commands the cadence. She commands the vibration, the temperament, and the texture. Oh God, her textures! Every gesture tickles the chords like a court jester, bountiful as laughter from her throat. She can make a song somber; and she can make a song giddy. But the song, *don't mean a thing if it ain't got that swing! Doo-wop, doo-wop, doo-wop...* Her body so fat with talent that the whole room protrudes. And we are so enraptured by her volcanic eruptions, that we all become ash-covered statues. Completely classic, persuasively pushing us over with her seductive blues. We are exhilarated by you, Ella Fitzgerald, so I am paying this tribute to you.

Era of Music Haiku

It grooves me and
soothes A treat, mellow
or upbeat Nineties RnB

Summer Breeze

Chorus Summer Breeze makes me feel fine, flowing through the jasmine in my mind.

Oven baked like ceramics, cream colored and dynamic in my view heat in my gaze strong enough to tint you hue. I spotted you. I mean I locked in my scope and put my hope in you. I sorted through the logistics to accumulate the equation that added me to you that added us to the collage, the exhibit, the montage of *Lovers' Lane* I made it sane in my brain and explain it to anyone who might ask or interrogate.

Brotha, I investigated you like the CIA. I put a poster of you up on the walls of my mind for display. Each night I would replay every step that I took toward you. My mind manipulated that fantasy until us became true.

But even that wasn't identical to the episode that would unfold as we took our journey through time, flowing through the jasmine in my mind- flowing through the jasmine in my mind.

Reality is the hardest thing to find when caught in the maze of a dream. I keep staring at this cream-colored figure. He seems to come alive and dance with me in the scene of this midnight extravaganza. We tango and two-step. Our feet speak a melodic stanza. We become grandeur inviting the allure of the rhythm to draw us closer, and closer to rapture. But alas, I find that you are not my possession and therefore you can never be captured or enclosed in my grips. And the lips of your mouth will never whisper, "I love you" in my presence.

Nor will our conversation ever become more than casual, or pleasant in passing. The currents of everlasting will never set our masses to passing as we transport on our journey through time. But you will forever be the jasmine in my mind. Boy, you are the jasmine in my mind, because...

Summerbreeze makes me feel fine, flowing through the jasmine in my mind.

Bad Boy:
A Tribute to Luther Vandross

Tip toe past in Stacy Adams through the grass Head bowed low, moving slowly slyly. Hoping mama doesn't see through the window seal. The electricity in the air is real. He can feel the zeal. Creeping up through his oily cocoa skin He's out to steal hearts and win numbers. Slick conversation and tricks up his satin sleeve He is a bad boy making all the ladies believe. He's only got eyes for them and them alone laser focused and in the zone. Owning the moment. Seizing the sizzling night with ready hands and roaming eyes like strobe lights. Opportunities bright and abounding. Lips looking luscious and gaze full of wanderlust. Wondering where the nearest basement party might be. Wondering if there is a popping disco tech to set his young body free I'm wondering if he will save a dance for me, teenage me. Cause we're having a party. Dimly lit and volume high. *We're having a party* and all the cool kids are inside. Swaying and sweating. Fish jumping, cotton high. We're having scatting a jazzy funky good time. Luther's velour voice playing in the background. *We're having a party* and everyone is getting down

Whip
Appeal

You had my head oscillating like a fan. You blew me
away with your chill vibe. This is just a poem to describe
the cool in you. Your tenor tone is so tender. You add
the delicate, yet indelible touch to my favorite genre. It's
exactly what my soul needs.

I cherish your family's legacy of beautiful bravado to vibrate my speakers into the

wee hours. There is so much complexity to you, Kenney. The beauty began with LA

Reid, Arista Records 1989. And you've continued this musical odyssey for over three

decades with a graceful stride. You make the lyrics come alive when you strum a

guitar or caress the ivories. You make melodies in color soar through the heavenlies.

You're such a musical visionary. Your notes wrap around the wind and
penetrate the heart as they descend. You are always suited sharp with
LAFace chiseled features, decadent and dark. A gentleman that meets
the mark with classic jams that become a work of art. This tribute is just
a small part to describe the cool in you.

For Will,
Drive

Key in the ignition, put it into drive. I know
you'll be right there when I arrive.
Something about this music keeps me
alive. You are the muse. Light the fuse for
the scribe. Whenever I'm zoning, I can
keep flowing. I can keep going

Verse

1

Moon aglow, haloed cloud-covered lover. You light the pathway, lead me
to discover another melody, another midnight summer breeze. I escape
from the darkness into your delicate reach. Each time I ponder, let my
thoughts saunter, encounter me at every intersection. Cosmic GPS the way
you encompass my direction. No more wandering. You're pinpointing to
self-expression. On the expressway I'm a blazing meteorite en route to a
session. Whiz by, a speeding zephyr, spit something clever, tickle the ear
like feathers, cadence to the measure tethered to my tongue. I feel it on-the-
one, release it on the two. By three, I'm elevated interstellar rearview.
Started on the interstate, ended on the moon. Charting halfway to
heaven. Set your telescope to zoom.

Verse

3

Gaze deeper into the lens as the volume ascends. We can attend the horizon as the orchestra of nature begins. Rend the silence from the firmament and climb the scale as beauty prevails. Notes trail ride the tail of a comet. Cosmic rays chase the shade away. A ballet of light arabesques across darkness. The artists digest the visage recants the display. The artist digests the visage, recants the display. You could say that the masterpiece speaks to the reality around. You hear the majesty peak from the speakers, bleed sound! When the world goes down to slumber, is when my mind begins to design the wonder. Sample the musical flavors. If you are what you eat, I'm such a tasty creator. Innovator, Originator, Smooth Operator stage to the paper. Ink drips treasured thoughts from my lips. Yeah, yeah.

Outro

4 beats to a measure, four wheels to the ride, my sole applies pressure 4-wheel drive. 4/1 to resolve it. 4/1 to arrive, imperfectly evolved, 4-wheel drive.

Soul
Baker

Angelic songstress Body &

Soul croons and rocks:

Anita Baker

Fireworks ascending. Scaled snow-capped mountains peaks. Time-lapsed Houston skyline. Water droplets off a soaked red rose. Windblown desert sands. Steep Icelandic terrains. Tide bursting onto oceanfront. Smoke dancing in front of an onyx backdrop. Raging flames, coursing in a carousel.

All of these scenes rushed on the screen behind the petite
queen.

Your voice heavy and deep. Your voice buttercream. Your soul incandescently leaped into every inch of the scenery. I was taken with your sequins sparkle. I was dazzled and dazed. I was exalted as my hands raised into the air; we swayed with you. The pianist played. Decades full of great hits came from the arcade of your open mouth feeding our famished memories. Our senses were full of you, our minds euphoric. You made our *love fly free* for old times' sake. You became the quake in the cavernous depth of our hearts. Two rows in front of me, I saw a man unexpectedly drop down to one knee. She gave a teary-eyed, 'yes.' Loved ones swooped in as cranes descending flight, wingspans elongated to express congratulatory hugs. Anita, your voice fit snugly into the moment. Your song was the catalyst that sparked this proposal. You plugged your cries into the auditorium, a live fuse to our circuitry. We were fully charged with you. Your songs ran through and through *from beginning to end, 365* ways.

Poetry According to Philippians 1:6

Chorus   According to, according to, according to, according to
poetry

Verse   God's work in human hands: May we be worthy of the pen we hold,
submissive as a sacrificial lamb. Call it Holy Communion, bold as the ink
drops.

The culture pops effervescently, by motto and
creed.

The blood never recedes, only goes silent momentarily.

In the interim when the time comes please supply us with everything we
need.

Please quail the intrigue for the allure of the flesh, grant us the anointing to
bless.

Let your light emanate through our skin to
manifest.

May molars and incisors chew on the fat of you and digest
this truth.

Succulent and satisfying as stewed meat or anything smothered
in gravy.

I am covered in clay, Lord, and loving the way you
made me.

Through the living word you persuade me, woo me, prove
yourself to be my sufficiency.

This beauty is All
consuming.

My quill is trembling like feathers in the
breeze.

My mind can't keep up with this delicate writing my hand is
scribing.

I do believe my heart knows and has always
known what the divine has shone upon like
the dawn.

Saffron and marigold, scarlet and yellow, ambers and
halo – your love flows like a river into my palm,
saturates these psalms.

In the still and quiet calm hours of sleep you creep into my heart
songs.

You sneak into my conversations with elders, you slip into my
steeping tea, you snuggle your way into my intimacy with like-
minded human beings.

You serenade me with wisdom that you've stored up for such a time as this.

You bid me to speak your words, and forbid me to remain silent... so how could I resist?

You've entrusted me with your parchment in hand; because through me YOU KNOW YOU CAN complete the work.

For He who began a good work *in you will carry it through.*

Jazzy Haiku 1 & 2

1. Her walk is sultry.

Each brass band serenade

step leaves the men

gasping.

Her legs are polished. Bronze

colored instruments glide a

trombone solo.

2. Saxophone sexy,

pressure builds upon his

reed. The man blows his

cool.

When he sees her walk

the melody finds blue

note. Jazz is seduction.

A Poem for Sarah Vaughn

Sarah Vaughn led them down a 'Misty' path traipsing toward the bliss of duet. The band struck midnight... bathed them in moonlight. Quincy's tailor suited bow casting a suave silhouette. The music didn't end there. Romance found a fanfare. Love is the lingering type with a song all its own.

      The trombone slides to a saxophone rise: An intimate tune to lead them home.

Oceans
Tanka

Inspired by Hillsong United
Oceans

Levitate on faith Walk on
water, wading hope. Keep
your eyes on Christ. Waves
can't wash away focus.
Doubt sinks in His saving
gaze.

Somewhere between us. Stands
sand prints and sinner's prayers. I
have stored up trust. Oceans of
adversity. Won't crush my
sandcastle faith.

Salt, water, in blood Grains.
of sand on my body.
Interconnection I am a
walking ocean. The depth of
me stems from you

Miss Calypso

I never knew God was a ventriloquist, until the 1st time your lips parted within my range of vibration. Ribbons of prismatic beauty began flowing from your soft-spoken conversation. As all the sequestered seraphim hushed from their "Hallelujahs" and adamantly took heed. The universe inclined itself brimming from anticipation on bended knee, thirsting for living waters to spring.

You then, proceeded with ancient dialog, sung out with a contemporary citrus twist. You sat and unraveled truth from gray coils of hair entwined within each gentle wisp.

You were perched their looking regal in your chair, sharing sacred jewels and spools of golden thread. I began to wonder were there mystic philosophers trapped inside of your head, whispering mantras and enchantment in glowing chromatic beads.

You laid out strands and strings, bear from breath to breath. Shook my soul 'til nothing was left, but awe-struck silence. Violets and blue-indigos created a spectrum of Crayola colors, painted so intentional, syllable after syllable.

You let loose a rainbow, parted my cumulus clouds of ignorance. If we could crack the sky wide open, we'd see God's mouth moving a pantomime of rhythm to your tongue and cheeks. You were his mouthpiece, when the grasp of understanding was too far beyond our reach. Maya you kept all of God's secrets until you were told to speak. You clutched his wisdom, until you were commanded to teach.

You were a modern-day disciple and the arts were you medium of speech. *Miss Calypso*, may I call you, 'Queen?' You mamboed your way into our minds speaking the mother tongue of many lands. With a red dressed shimmy, you became the saffron in the summer breeze, the coconut milk in our rice and peas.

The effervescent pooling of water stirred in the belly of gospel. Your impact on literature is so colossal! History pages will forever whisper your name an apostle of

prose, of lyric, and of psalm.
From the heavens to the earth your legacy
lives on.

Formulating
Fantasia

The wand wavers in his hand with star dust bathing the tip and drifting off into expectant space. His pointed hat pierces the air around it. Dandelion seeds of light whimsically dance off the blue-violet cone shape.

Tonight, a symphony of alchemist grace will orchestrate a magical production. Tonight, he stands robed in red rare form taking center stage. He ascends the pinnacle of the galaxy calling mystery into existence. He is the magician curating with harmonious gestures. A well-lit overture lifts from his stick slicing through the air with rhythmic bursts of beauty.

The universe knows no bounds between each bar, each measure, for with each beat, he gathers white gloved momentum.

> Like a pendulum arcing high and gliding
> down, optical illusions merge with occipital
> reality.

A mouse muses with the music, index fingertip extends to exuberance. He flings rays of light. He directs buckets and brooms throughout the night, the constellations and a bricked cauldron booming right beneath his command.

He is pointing with purpose and poise and all of the universe understands his fanfare. He has formulated the fantasia with the mind of a magician and his mousy little hands.

Sweet Nostalgia

This is one of those Pete Rock C.L. Smooth kind of
grooves. Where emotions choke you up as your head
starts to move. Thinking back like Ahmad... remember
way back when? I'm talking plastic couch covers
grandma's house in the den. Rap city the basement.
Big Lez and Joe Claire, Tiger in the booth freestylin'.

Let my words take you there. When the glare of hip
hop shined brighter than the sun. Wu-Tang was on
the radio, Outkast & Big Pun. Some of the greatest
rappers have fallen. Some of the fallen are still alive.
Old skool can bring em' back. May the bass revive
'em. I miss when Common Sense was rooted in
consciousness. *Cotton Candy on a Rainy Day* kinda
bliss.

The spirit of nostalgia is a goddess. Her essence is so poetic.
I reminisce on her beauty, vibe so copasetic, inspiration, and
artistry. I flow with her aesthetic. No, I can't let it go. It would
burn like antiseptic.

Sweet Nostalgia starts gouging at my eye sockets
like a blast from the past shooting off like bottle
rockets Oh, Nostalgia, I can't live without ya.
Sweet Nostalgia, I can't live without you.

Ballad of a Lonely Girl

My heart dripped

sentiments His touch

grew intimate

But his fingers never found my

skin It was his words that drew

me in

The fervor in his gaze

Melted my hesitation

away

But he had no permanence He could

not stay: I could not persuade him

Love never goes my

way

Sweetest Taboo to
Love Deluxe

Hips, full lips, and soothsaying

 silken slip dress, and slicked back

hair

        freckles and flesh, every memory associated with your melody

seduces me. The way you undress sound slowly and glide your voice

             into my earlobes, that is to say, I cannot stop listening,

                because I am delighted by the sensations you

cause. My heart holds no applause. My voice lauds with you.

        I shower you in praise. Sade Adu, everything about

             you is on a pedestal in my mind.

                      I can find no reason to

refrain. You braise my soul in your sauce. You tempt me to skinny-dip in these

emotions.

             I could swim laps around your

             soulfulness.

                   Your eyes are my personal lost and

found. I rotate your track listing, body-rolling my torso to your basslines. I close my eyes

tightly, furrowed brow folding like Venetian blinds shutting out the sun.

             Your voice takes me dark. Let's embark on this mood

together. My fingers snap along to the cadence.

         I am moaning for your moonlight. I am a

bloodhound sniffing out the pureness of your residence within any room.

When I pick up your scent, I am rent as the heavens like rain on a

sunny day. I am an addict since every yesterday that comes before

 today.

On a Sunday I sway, on a Monday I await, on a Tuesday I play, on a Wednesday I replay, on a Thursday I sway, on a Friday I wait, on a Saturday all I can say is *Look the sky is full of love.*

Just Another Jazz Poem 'cause it's

the easiest thing for me to write

Mr. Jazz man was scatting skittles
to me

rainbows bursting from his lips in vibrant
tones.

I was caught in the haze of harmony opening my mouth to a frenzied
vibration.

As my lips brushed up against his tenor with my
alto...

Slow was the
build.

Legato was the
flow.

No, we never let go of this sweet
confection.

We kept building until the bridge could carry us
over

towards the direction of a brighter
horizon.

We shouldered this music in our mouths like it was our mantle our very birthright.

The piano became our midwife as our song was born that night.

We inhaled deep Lamaze breaths, let the melody pour from our chest... panting as we pressed.

Selah

Amy Winehouse Haiku

She wears Merlot like it's
a lip stain. She takes sips
A ballad is born.

Take me *Back to*
Black, A record
reminiscent. Classic
soul reborn.

Ask The
River

Chorus

> *I spoke to the river. I had so much to*
> *say.*
> *I talked to the river. She answered me in*
> *waves.*

Verse

1

I once asked the water, "Do you recognize me?" My whole body, a river, frame that flows and ripples deep within coursing to currents of beauty. Liquid hearth gurgling with inseparable droplets and always inviting My entire habitat encompassing Salted and fresh, full, and rushing with life. Never damned, or receding, and certainly never stagnant. My movement a fluid feminine rhythm, trickling or hasty, through valleys and mountains I wind. I am no pond. Yet at times, I resemble an ocean.

I once asked the water, "Do you recognize me?" I sat still, waited for an answer, All I saw was my reflection in the fluxes of waves.

Chorus

I spoke to the river. I had so much to say.

I talked to the river. She answered me in waves.

Whitney Houston
Haiku

Palace of silence the
kingdom of music weeps
soft song of lament

Drowning melody Sink to
the surface of death. Her
memory floats.

Ms. Moses
In Concert

She is a songbird serenading us with silky selections Tune is
perfection. Takes me back to the place when I fell in love with music.
I've anticipated tonight with haste. Found a place in my heart where
palpitations and melodies collide. This *Complex Simplicity* is a
masterpiece in the making. She is a muse of expression, mesmerizing
and engaging us with her melisma. She opts to croon the minor,
jazzes up the spectrum. She finds a new hue for rhythm and blues. I
am too taken aback to bundle my joy. There is no coy form of ovation.
There is a surging exclamation that overflows from the throats of
those looking on at her artistry. We are entertained by the beauty of
being beheld, being regaled, being the recipients of a truly benevolent
nightingale.

Upholding

She arose from the raw earth, the color of dirt leftover. Rotating sphere on her shoulders, she's been carrying this 3rd rock boulder, reclaiming mass, getting older. Yet remaining unclassified and marginalized trying to justify the legitimacy of her craft.

Like an epigone uttering under an overpass, in a state of repose. She is spouting golden-tinted prose in the shadows abscising truth from lies. She's quoting poets and philosophers of the past, maturity personified in her overcast skies.

Even so, those glittering pools are still luminous bright. She takes big bites of palatable light. Recites and regurgitates. She has quantified wisdom beneath the guise of charisma, charm, and colloquialism wrapped in wit.

Despite the prize that she is, often times, she's cast aside and disregarded. Simply because most cannot handle it. Their bellies poisoned by propaganda. She holds the anecdote in her sweet sticky stanzas. Each light lick-able lyric that leaps from her tongue leaves their egos undone. Leaves their privilege in the spillage of her tongue. They are livid from how she pillages their ignorance with just one proverb.

She has come from the asylum of assemblies to massacre them with her innate abilities. Originated from epics of lore, all her glory can never be truly accounted for. The ancestors just keep rising in her bones. God's fire is what is shut up in her bones. Her mystique is somewhere between renaissance and *Love Jones*.

She is imitated, under-appreciated, appropriated but never truly owned. They cannot hone. They cannot harness. They can only hope to clone. But her chromosomes are sacred and the sacrifice that it took to comprise her genetic code cannot be duplicated. She is in and of herself one of a kind; and in a class of her own.

She stands alone, holding up her portion of this raw earth. She is a million times worth more than has been accounted for. And as long as she lives, she will always have more left over to give.

She manifests in
abundance. She
manifests abundance.

Prickly

Prickly passion penetrates pretty epidermis. She keeps posturing her spine to receive this thistle and thorny embrace. She doesn't perceive the hostility with which it comes pressing so fervently into her flesh. She is obliviously loving, recklessly and relentlessly loving. She sacrificed herself with scarlet blood hugging her curves trickling to the desert sand mixed with the moisture of her passion.

This love hurts so good. Grief, she wonders why she is suddenly weak. Wonders why she is punctured and paralyzed to the point of immobility. It seems she didn't recognize the sharp, didn't discern the blades. She was too confused and focused on the lush. She was looking past the damaging daggers to the shade of smoothness on her lovers' stem. She kept reaching for the flowering bud. She kept seeking pedals and skin. So much so, that she made her body bend to every needle point that came pushing in. Silly woman didn't realize that cacti have no heart. Silly woman couldn't comprehend that her copious watering was unwanted and not needed for this prickly plant to grow.

Yet and still she loved it so. *You're so sharp you pierce me, You're so sharp. You're prickly.*

Rap

No warning shots. Just thorn of thought, bleeding profusely. No blood clots. I'm not saying that you used me. But have you ever hugged a porcupine? Have you ever pulled a quill from your spine? I can read the warning signs loud a clear. The red is flashing stop, whenever you are near. I'm heading for the walls and barricades. Love cuts me deep just like a blade, like a blade.

Beautiful
Creation

I attune to 432

megahertz.

Create God's work in a kente skirt. Blurt out truth to

attract virtue. The composition of intuition seek

harmony in a prism of blue.

I'm tryin' to feel the vibe from you, based on your

resonance.

Let love proceed from me and establish

precedence.

It's truly a gift to be

present.

Unwrapping my frequency real time, fully aligned, becoming

aware, giving, thread to this tapestry, shedding my soul and

my light bare.

We can share the best parts of our art when

we care. Kiss the concentrated self, feel the

trembling there.

Let the negativity crumble. I do not digress. I use every breath

to needle press this spooling material into substance. Every

particle of my sub tense supports the arc in my wavelength,

giving strength to my vibration. Fortify the fibers of my Soul

Physics.

Examine it. Ain't that a

beautiful creation?

We are all just oxygenated vessels, couriers of electricity and

impulse. Our heart rate pulsates to the rhythm of respirations.

(palpitating) We are all breathing the same airwaves, particles of

energy. We are all taking in the same sun rays that sustain life,

absorbing light.

Let the magnetism draw you in. Float to me

like hydrogen. Like electrons orbiting,

cosmic as a space station.

And again I ask you, ain't it a beautiful

creation? I ask you, a beautiful creation.

I
Wish

I could map these stars 'til they shoot out the sky. I
could cast my coins in wells to pile a mountain
high. I could blow out candles to save my life from
shambles. I'll try

I prayed for you. I waited for you. I longed for
you, to make my dreams come true.

I hoped for
you

I wished for
you.
I have wanted you to make my life feel brand
new Ooh and I wish and I wish

Traverse the universe on pins and needles,
collecting scarab beetle shells. Peek into the
universe with hope to see where angels dwell.
One never plans to fail, but the travail of rebirth
is hell on earth. We feel the labor pains
beneath our skin and skirts. Imagine being so

desperate to break from human chains.

It

hurts.

We try tremendously to put our plans to work. Dig
wells in the dirt then cast our change into infinity.
Longing and wishing, hoping, desiring our fate will
meet good fortune, for the future we're admiring,
until we're elevated with higher beings truly
overseeing, without perspiring.

Sweat it out.
Then, let it
out.

Push hard and get it
out. Push hard, then
get it out.

Vamp

There's no genie in a lamp, no lamp to
rub. No wish bones to break. I feel out
of luck, fresh out of luck. There's no
genie in a lamp, no lamp to rub, no
wish bones to break.

But I can't give up, no. I can't give

up. And I wish, and I wish, I wish.

Oooo.

She Tastes Like Music

Thoughts of sweet melody run down my
tongue. Can't get enough, tastes like my
favorite song. Harmony pallets my senses
undone. She tastes like music

Verse

1

Nourishment from a fine specimen, sustenance oozing out from
her pigmentation. She could feed the nation delectable
creations of the highest vibration. Body dialed up like a radio
station. She ain't handing out samples But Brothers stay
waiting. Salivating for her melody. Tastes so heavenly. Man,
you better be ready 'cause her tracks are stacked with phat
beats and in heavy rotation flavors so elating, titillating. She
satiating taste buds with the purest drug. All hail the empress;
you can taste the love. Wrap your tongue around her tune. Let
it melt in your mouth, hot as June. (Avidly Consumed.)

Verse

2

Arpeggio crowning her tempo. She is adorned in harmony let
her bless you with her iridescent glow. It's so saucy on her skin.
Like the refraction of light off the surface. She has risen even
when muted tones would try to color her worthless. And the
savory taste of her virtue has thickened like a roux She's made

of muddy waters, swampy like the bayou. You've never heard the blues until you nibbled on her neck. And you never knew the rhythm 'til her lips gave you a peck. She can rock and roll you or slather jazz across the tongue. Every genre: you will lick it, you will like – every single one.

Jazz That
I Am

I be that saxophone. I be that trombone. I be that jazz song. My voice is a microphone. I am piano keys. My walk is a symphony. My heels click like a tambourine. Music is my every, everything. Give me jazz, jazz that I am. Give me jazz, jazz that-I-am. Give me jazz, jazz that I am. I, aye, aye aye aye am jazz...

Give me a Thelonius Monk kind of funk, to smooth my wrinkled morning blues. Cruise down my memory bank with subdued bebop bruised melodies. Rain down my soul, from the heavenlies, fat cold drops of precipitation. I think my flesh was awaiting its creation through Coltrane stained saxophone notes chained to clay and Adam's missing rib. As Dizzy Gillespie caressed me, molded and shaped me to supple trumpet toots. The bravado of my heart began to shoot through the roof of my mouth; and a jazzy phat nasty sound came spouting out. I let the pitch of it shout over Kenny Clarke, drum taps having a musical spat with the rainbow in my smile. And for a while, I drowned my mind in the lines of an old Louis Armstrong, song as the breath of his cheeks pushed me along. From then on, I knew my spirit belonged with Dexter Gordon greats. So file me among the ranks with Charlie Parker and Johnnie Hodges, as their instrumental music massages my temples, changing the tempo of my thoughts. Lately, I have been dwelling on Duke Ellington keystrokes. Mental images float off his elegance and with relevance promote my thought patterns to linger-- in limbo with Nina Simone. As, Cab Calloway echoes his resonance of a *Hi-de-hi-de-hi-de- HOOOO.* Twirling in a yellow pinstripe zoot suit with matching hat to boot. I tell you, I am a recruit for a jazzy dream team. So stream me through Doc Perry's piano pounding. Gleam me in a montage of cool and big band swing. Whirl me on the surface of a melodic color scheme, Harlem mahoganies and dutch D.C. chocolate browns. Catch me in this movement of symphonic sound. And I will never come down from the very high found in my blood as it pumps. So, give me a Thelonius Monk kind of funk.

A true black Billie Holiday groove. A luscious Lena Horne tune. A croon from Sarah Vaughn to spawn a midmorning press for my bunchy blues. Cause I want to be smooth so smooth. As jazz, is jazz a renovated soul, innovated from old, and inundated with cold drops of rain. Just as inflamed as they... carnivorously drunk with this neo classic, Thelonious Monk kind of funk. So say it to me, give it to me. Live it through me. SAY IT TO ME, play it through me. I am a significant infant, adolescent, to emanate woman projecting and expressing this air inspired artform. My body performs it every mi-nute minute of every passing day. For three decades and seven years you can hear me jazz. Wood wind, percussion, string with discussion, BRASS. Like is, baby I am: containing, becoming, and being pizzaz. And I have-as-much-as, with such class... A Thelonious Monk, kind of funk jazz, ja-ah-ah-zz, jazz... That I am. mmm

Simply
Me

Woke up to an epiphany of who I've become:
The embodiment of my experiences,
coupled with temperance emanated into this song.

I know right where I belong.

Tucked underneath my skin is the perfect
blend: Grace, wisdom & certainty. My
affirmations match my expectations. My
whole body is an anthem. My heartbeat
keeps the drum. It's so amazing!

Feeling lush virtuosity. It's
amazing, the blend of fabric
woven meticulously.

I see the good in
me.

Natural beauty internally, it flows
through fluidly like fine linens of self-
love. Esteeming my heart in high regard
looking above fault lines. No more
earthquakes of criticism & critique.
Won't weigh myself against others.

I am

unique.

Endnotes

Queen of Swing: the word ba·lay·age : a technique for highlighting the hair in which the dye is painted on in such a way as to create a graduated, natural-looking effect. In this case, the stage light is highlighting Ella.

Poetry According to Philippians 1:6 was inspired thrice: by my favorite Talaam Acey poem, holy scripture, and a transcendent night of jazz music at Tony G's please look them up on youtube: The Murray El'Zabar Project. I was honored to be able to view their work, open for them, and get in on some improv with them while I was in the room.

She Tastes Like Music: This is the title track for the album, the lyrics are heavily cadence driven and rhythmic. The piece is speaking to music as the muse and the flavor of a woman that centers her life around harmony and balance. It is her metaphor. It adds all of the excitement and mood to the pace of her life. The piece views music as a layered experience that covers the entire spectrum of the five senses. *(Chorus written by Nigel Slaughter)*

Upholding: This piece is a third person description of myself, and the personification of primary subject throughout this project. "She," is a woman that is has faced numerous accounts of discrimination yet endured and overcome. This piece speaks to the ability to maneuver within culture and society and use disadvantages to learn lessons and be resourceful. It also speaks to genetic memory calling upon what has been passed down from diaspora to present day. It is a piece that speaks to creating space for oneself no matter the climate: economically, class, academically, and in all environments.

Invocation to Sun Ra and *Origins of a Arkestra Leader* came about because I did a Sun Ra tribute at Southwest School of the Arts with the legendary Nick Long of the band Lonely Horse and Xavier Gilmore, as a part of his Astro Black exhibition. This experimental goodness is documented on YouTube in a "Boosh Session."

Soul Baker: July 1, 2019 I witnessed Anita Baker's farewell tour in Sugarland, TX. For those hours, she gave us the best that she had.

Duet (*Kind of Blue* and *All Blues*): these poems came about because my buddy Adam Tutor, put together a tribute to Miles Davis, classic and timeless album *Blue in Green*, released in 1959. I decided to put them together in the book as a duet because they are meant to be read back to back.

Jazzy Jeff is a dedication to my mentor in poetry, Charles "Easy Lee" Peters, who asked me to co- author/colab on a song. We never got around to recording that joint. But makes a comparison to the relationship that Jazzy Jeff and Jill Scott have being similar to the friendship that him and I share. You all should just get into Mojoe's music those boys are fiyah! Their debut is entitled *Classic Ghetto Soul*, released in 2006.

Bass in Between came about, not because I have a personal affinity for bassist, Charlie Mingus. But because I have a great saxophonist friend named George Briscoe, who once heard me perform *Jazz that I Am*, he was very concerned that I left Mr. Mingus out of that poem. He asked me to write an entire piece about Charlie or add him to the poem. So with George in mind, I set out to do just that. It was years before George ever heard me recite the poem. Every time I would show up to slam to perform it, he was M.I.A. Overall, would like to add George Briscoe is a faithful attendee of Puro Slam, a long running slam hosted by Jason "Shaggy" Gossard. I am the one that was rarely there.

Prickly has a cool little backstory. I was inspired by a picture I took during a photoshoot with B. Kay Richter at the Botanical Gardens. I was in the desert climate room and posed by some cacti. I decided to post the picture on Instagram and wrote a little personal poem. I later decided to record it on a whim with no music behind it. A few weeks later, I submitted that poem for publishing through the website Submittable.com (writers check it out if you don't have an account) I found an audio submission for *Anti-Languorous Project*. They accepted my submission and published me in, *Soundbite Vol 3*. I am the only non-Canadian published in that issue. I talked to Jeff Palacios, my good friend that produced the track for the song after hearing the dry audio, and decided to keep the entire beat he made. So *Prickly* is the longest song on my album and features the vocals of incomparable Solis and L.Q. Iverson. L.Q. engineered almost my entire album in his studio.

Simply Me this poem and song, I cannot take full credit for due to the fact that it is the title track from an artist out of London, Adelaide MacKenzie. This song appears on her album as the title track and also on my album. I am proud to have had the honor of collaborating with this extremely talented woman, whom I have never met in person. Her speaking voice I liken to a blanket fresh out of the dryer. I wish I was born with her accent.

Acknowledgements

First and foremost, I am here with a rapid heartbeat and icy cold fingers trying to make sure I say all of the things from my heart to express my love and gratitude towards God the Father, Son and Holy Spirit, for telling me to do my part, and they would make the rest happen. Where to begin? Artist Foundation of San Antonio and the Tobin Center of Performing Arts, you are the reason why this project has seen the light of day in an elevated and expedient manner, better than I could have accomplished on my own. Special thanks to: Edward Vidarrue and my Flower Song Books family and all of the RGV poets hanging out by the border. Jo Reyes-Boitel and Dominique Edmonds, thank you for the painstaking hours of enduring my neurotic mind changes and quirky discontent. Mac's Visionary Dreams for all the love you put into creating color around me, I am grateful. Tamara Adira of *Arte y Pasión*, you are such a clear visionary and my heart is glad that over the past two years, I have had the pleasure of calling you my close friend and comrade. You have encouraged my craft and execution. You have taught me a new rhythm and culturally enriched my heart with awareness. Thank you for making me, "George Bush," the button and send off my grant proposal. Xelena Gonzalez, you ma'am, literally blow my mind with your excellence!! How do you even do it all and take dance breaks in between your stellar accomplishments? Laura Van Prooyen, thank you for so many chats and hugs along this process. We did it!!

Dulcie, my bestie, I have really enjoyed hearing you speak about how educators in H.I.S.D. are going to benefit from all of this self-care and pursuing their own writing careers. I am proud of you for working on your manuscript and I cannot wait to see you published! Zach Jewell, Ami Nah, George (*Tree of Life Fine Arts Education*) Thank you for the encouragement and prayers along the way.

Gylon Jackson, Glo Armmer, Kinton Armmer, Kevin Mr. Composition Prince, Paula of *Carmen's De La Calle*, Lauren Browning and Kinyo Laditan of *GET*, every single one of you are instrumental in partnering with me over the years. Thank you: Francisco Cortes, B. Kay, and Alejandra Sol Casas, Nicole Marie Moore, and Tony Polanco - I appreciate you for capturing beautiful moments through your lens.

Gemini Ink and Bexar County Juvenile Detention Center staff, especially Liz Stafford-Baldwin (my precious mommy) Arnisha & Joshua, Steven Fletcher Jr. and Florinda Flores Brown, you all are my support pillars. It is really great to feel supported by my co-workers and bosses while I spend so much time creating space for myself. You all have given me the freedom to do so. Charles Peters, Naomi Shihab Nye, Claudio San Miguel, Octavio Quintanilla,Jim La Villa-LaHavelin and Kalia Hpaeoati thank you all for giving me your words and thoughts of honesty as I navigate this process. Your wisdom is a clear beacon. Thank you Bernita Ward for your nuggets of wisdom. Thank you, to Neka and Tha1Radio, 91.7 Kory Cook, JJ Lopez and all the KRTU folks, 90.1 KSYM. Chris Conde and all the lovely people at *The SA Current*, your journalism is a full spectrum enlightening the citizens of San Antonio. The Foreign Arm my band of 5 years and all the members we've had over the years, you all gave me a gift of friendship and music that is massive in so many ways.

Thank you to all of *Mc2 & Tha S.O.U.L.* Debra Elana, Nicholas Blevins, Nigel Pierce, Solis, L.Q. Iverson, Keith 'Smeazy' Passmore, Beatowski, Jonathan Terrell, Jamail Chachare, Nick Shan, Donnie Singleton, Ricky Castro-Harris, Mark Crawford, Adelaide McKenzie, Mykal Max, and Jeff Palacios for putting your hands to the creation of *She Tastes Like Music*. 2nd Verse Open Mic, Blah Poetry, Puro, Barrio Barista, Sun Poets, Jazz Poets, Jazz & Poetry with a Purpose, Dream Week Dream Voice, Aaron Prado trio, Rene Saenz Quartet, the patrons of the arts, donors, sponsors, anyone who has attended, followed me, (Eman Cipate & Ami Nah) you all are loved and adored. I cannot name you all, but I love you.

Special thanks to my poppa Arthur Sanderson, aka DJ Daddy Old Skool. I inherited my love of music from you. Your passion for creating the perfect mix makes my heart flutter like an 8-track. I owe so much of who I am to you.

Author Bio

Andrea Sanderson performs as "Vocab" in her hometown of San Antonio, Texas. "Watching her perform, the word "hero" comes to mind. Not "hero" for the sake of just skill, but for her work in her community: Sanderson teaches poetry workshops, mentors, builds up and encourages artists to pursue their art, and gives them platforms to showcase their talent.

"Sanderson's interest in other people's art and artistic development became a passion of hers, and she started curating her own shows and creating platforms for other artists to hone their craft by hosting open mics." (*From The San Antonio Current*, Jan. 16, 2018.) She is the co-host of 2nd Verse Open Mic and Jazz & Poetry with a Purpose. She began organizing emerging artist showcases in 2007 with an event called, *Soul Portico*. In March of 2018, she assembled an all women cast for a sold-out theatre show, *The Bad Mama Jama Mixtape: A Woman's Soundtrack to Life*, at the historical *Little Carver*. Andrea is also an arts educator, and began teaching creative writing workshops in 2008. She has traveled as far as, Abu Dhabi (2015), sharing her knowledge with the troops stationed there.

Her poetry is published in, *The Texas Observer*, January 2016 Issue, *Pariah Anthology SFA Press*, March 2016, and *Sycorax's Daughters, Cedar Grove Publishing*, January 2017. She released a long anticipated single, "*Waiting For Me*," in December 2017.

She received the awards, *Performer of the Year, Influencer of the Year*, from Project Forward, and *Dream Voice*, from the Dream Week Commission; and most recently *The People's Choice Award* granted by Artist Foundation of San Antonio. In 2019 as part of her Artist Foundation Grant she released, *She Tastes Like Music*.

Purchase the companion CD, *She Tastes Like Music*, on www.andreavocabsanderson.com or digital music streaming platforms.

Printed in the USA
CPSIA information can be obtained
at www.ICGtesting.com
LVHW052125270723
753505LV00005B/406

9 781734 561715